Missing the Eclipse

JOAN HEWITT

Published by Cinnamon Press
Meirion House,
Glan yr afon,
Tanygrisiau,
Blaenau Ffestiniog
Gwynedd LL41 3SU.
www.cinnamonpress.com

ISBN: 978-1-905614-36-3

British Library Cataloguing in Publication Data. A CIP record for this book can be obtained from the British Library.

Designed and typeset in Palatino by Cinnamon Press
Cover design by Mike Fortune-Wood from original artwork 'Blood Moon' by Frank Boellmann, agency: dreamstime.com
Printed in Norfolk by Biddles, Ltd.

Acknowledgements

Versions of some of these poems have appeared in *London Magazine* and *Mslexia*; and in *Envoi* 's gala edition, June, 2008; in *Magnetic North*: New Work from North East Writers, (New Writing North,2005); in *100 Island Poems* of Great Britain and Ireland (Iron Press, 2005.); and in *Under My Skin*, an anthology of work from the MA in Writing Poetry, University of Newcastle,2003. 'Proof' and 'Reading Between the Lines' appear in *The Body and the Book: Writings on Poetry and Sexualit,*: Rodolpi Press, 2008

'Bareback Act' came joint second in the 2003 Ledbury International poetry competition. 'Evening, Unsettled' was a runner-up in the 2004 *Mslexia* poetry competition; as was 'Worm'. 'White' came third in the 2005 Sussex and Kent Open poetry competition and was poem of the month, June, 2007, for Diamond Twig publications. In 2004, a version of 'Double Exposure' ('Dock Road') came third in the Southport Open Poetry competition, and 'Lust Meadow' was third in the Lingham's Bookshop competition.

I am grateful to *New Writing North* for the 2003 Andrew Waterhouse Northern Promise Poetry Award, and, in conjunction with the Cultural Skills Partnership, for allowing me the skilful mentorship of poet Linda France.

Special thanks to poets Jake Polley, WN Herbert and Paul Farley for time, close reading, and advice on the shaping of the book. To the other members of the Northern Poetry workshop, thanks for the focused criticism, the friendship, and the fun.

Contents

for my daughters Laura, Anna and Kate;
and for Mark

with love

Missing the Eclipse

Act

Every day it's up and out of the marriage-bed
and its unfinished dreams, to leap straight on
the horse's waiting back. I touch my finger
to a spot midway between its blinkers,
and already my thighs are flexing, feet jabbing,
onward into the ring, where an old man
and three girls are seated for the breakfast turn.

At this hour, my breath's a grey flower
behind the horse's cloud. Straight
into first paces: grip; circle; bend backwards;
urge; and check. Breathe deep
as in a morning pranayama on damp sawdust,
toast, just-ironed cotton, strawberry lip-balm
and the piss in the pot left out for emptying.

We pick up rhythm quickly. Each twist
and stretch unchills the blood; flushes
the muscles and the brain of night-time's resins.
The canvas brightens and the tent begins to fill
with child-minders, neighbours, exchange students,
asylum-seekers, and union reps:
all in costume, working, or resting between acts.

Like sauna-steam, their body-heat
zings to my head and I'm off, I'm at it,
throwing stances, showing them a trick or two,
tilting my chin as I do the splits
or a sturdy one-legger on the horse's sweating back,
one arm curved delicately in upon itself
for me to admire its well-worked sinews.

Commuter Moon

She was high tonight, he saw at once
as he walked out of the station:
dilated, looming woozily towards him
away from the buttoned-up stars.
She had to be on something, to get herself
and the street so lit up and so perfect.

For once, doing the job, he thought,
avoiding her gaze. Blue lawns, long shadows,
rime on the roof of his house, cats on the wall
gleaming like ornaments. For his taste,
a little too film-set – the way she'd turned
his briefcase leather to patent, his coat to velvet –

even the luminous blonde hair of his daughter
running to meet him which, as he swung her,
fell cold as snow on his face. Behind her
the moon was too close and voluptuous.
Hard, closing the study door on their ache for approval,
but he had papers to read; an agenda to write.

At midnight, he went for a walk to unwind,
and found her still up by the pier,
blank, motionless over spectacular light.
Someone must have been at her,
then cleaned her up; dosed her. The sea
was a credit, though. A backdrop to nothing.

Proof

Finally, I took a photograph of myself
naked in the mirror taking a photograph
of myself naked in the mirror, for you.
I didn't send it. The camera-strap
skimming one nipple looked contrived,
and I threw it in the bin.

When I was with you, I remember
how it was easy to be natural.
Best fucking apple I ever ate,
you groaned as I moved off you.
Two sets of teeth-marks in the core,
a pip in the hollow of your neck.

Lately, I worry that you forget
what I am really like, and invent me
nightly out of telephone static,
distance, longing. I post
the video of me: baggy trousers,
cardigan and unwashed fringe.

Your letter back is lying on a bowl
of untouched fruit. *Thanks.*
I love it. Now stop doing this.
Tonight, go into the darkest room,
lie on the floor. Light the same candle.
Wait for my call.

Plotting

I was crouching on the road map in the living-room
when he rang. I told him *motorway, turn-off,*
twelve miles west, and *shouldn't be too easy*
– a slip he didn't notice .Then I said
he was from another planet. I meant
the way he moved his voice around inside me.

He rang off, and I saw that my bare foot
had inched north-west. Slowly, my toes
curled up to find the names: The Shin, Hollows,
Broad Head , Water of Milk. We might never
get there, but they made the bleakness of the route
– Scuggate, Haggbeck, Rough Pike – easier to ignore.

The Same Place Twice

This time it seems you haven't been completely celibate.
When you touch down at noon, butter wouldn't melt
in your familiar, eager mouth, but under your T-shirt
your skin could defrost peas in seconds.

You explain why letters stopped. In a rainstorm,
you'd reached in and grabbed the lever of the truck.
There was a bang. Lightning entered your writing hand,
coupling you briefly with a storm-cloud.

Things have happened since that can't be unconnected.
The house holds itself together – just – when you walk in.
The cat gets to you before me and offers you its stomach.
It isn't that you've changed. You're charged.

Hamlet's Ex-Wife

Marriage was perfect for soliloquies.
Meals, child-care arrangements and the deaths of pets:
the whole hullabaloo was just a backcloth.
And when his shadow fell across the birthday tea,
the cue for another speech to no-one but himself,
we all fell silent.

Well, he's gone.
The children are asleep, and centre-stage is cosy as the grave.
This could be just the break I need:
strong female lead, harsh lighting for pain
and courage, and sweet as breast-milk,
the audience attention.

I fix my eyes beyond the footlights
and try not to hear the rustling in the wings,
where the Hamlets are waiting.

Her Sense of Line

Over my lover's head
on the wall of his bedroom,
I see my daughter's present to him,
her painting of the fish-quay.

She mounted it herself
without the right equipment
and, under the polished glass,
the creases show.

In the hushed comfort
next to well-framed, brighter images,
its blues and greys
are cool as water.

The line never wavers.
Delicate and sure,
it reels me in, across the sea,
to her and home.

Comfort and Joy in Osterholz-Scharmbeck

We eat our cabbage at a round white table in the kitchen.
It is good and hot. The beer is good and cold.
Behind your parents' heads, framed in the oven door,
is an uncooked goose. The white cat stares.

On your room's pale carpet, under a square of window,
sex in snowlight is very, very good.
The soap to wash away its smells of forest
is liquid, scentless. The towels are warm and dry.

The whole house hums, wrapped round by snow.
I hum. On the glittering crunch of the Devil's Moor,
a sorbet between courses, we take a long walk
under a misty sun, a shaping moon.

A shot from a farmhouse turns our heads.
Firework, you say, *for New Year.* I imagine
soldiers and a man face down on the ground.
Between us a gap opens which I want us to be in.

When we get back, your mother has stripped the tree
and propped it naked in the garden. The lounge glows
chastely white. You spread goose-fat on dark bread
and watch the news: civilian casualties in Iraq.

Your father drives us to the airport. His new car
smells of plastic. On the *autobahn,* a thud.
No time to stop. From the heater, a stink of blood
and fur, almost to be savoured. You translate: *fox.*

Lust Meadow

She found a staun o' stauning graith
coming through the rye.

Die Lustwiese, your father called our bed,
which you had sawed and planed to take our weight
and anything we gave it, without a sound.
He translated sixty-four square feet of pine
into a dreamy negligence, shadows flitting over hay,
and the sweetness of nipped clover on the tongue.
The first night I had vertigo, hanging over the edge
to reach a glass. You swore but cut nine inches
off its legs; and, years later, swore again,
dismantling it for the move and labelling every screw.

It floats now in the ether of our room, strewn
with cloud pillows and white cotton, and we can have
each other any time we want, and well, except
at night when you are lost to Science Fiction.
This morning seagulls and a *Morgenlatte* wake you.
You fling your arm out and find beside you
cooling space; hear singing in the bathroom.
Gin a body meet a body comin' thro the rye,
Gin a body kiss a body, need a body cry ?
Shades of meadow vetch and ladies' mantle
play across your face. You call.

Tynemouth, 2003; *or* We Like It Here

The eggs are rattling in the pan
and the breakfast news is done.
On the patch of grass before the house,
the table's out. The cat
shows its stomach to the sun, and a child
is reaching through the fence to hold its paw.
We watch the trains, yellow and blue,
yellow and red, clank towards the town.

The ice is rattling in the jug.
We drink sloe gin
and read the evening paper. Our university
has banned all protests
against the war so that Iraqi students
can feel more secure. The rosebush
from our old house is rooting well.
A neighbour stops to ask if we feel settled in.

Failed Asylum Seeker: Attempted Re-entry

for Matvei

The cell door was opened, and he looked up.
There you are, he said.
The line around his throat was fresh; otherwise, he looked well.
The Idiot by Dostoevesky was lying on the bed.
He grinned.
Andrei's joke. He'd told me to try Ireland this time,
and I didn't know Belfast was the UK.

The customs guy who found him in the toilet and cut him down
said he was the first man he'd ever had to kiss.
Yes, he was working through my *Practical English Usage;*
he found double negatives and third conditionals difficult.

We sat down at the table to play chess.
I asked about the exercises for his back.
He shook his head.
No room to swing a cat in here. I looked that up.
Did you know 'cat' is an old Scottish word for thief?
No, I said. *You live and learn.*
He smiled and said he liked that one. Then moved his pawn.

Signs

for Laura; and Anna and Kate

Three hundred million years ago, this island
was nudging the equator, and took off
northwards on a whim, to shudder down
in rifts and seams in this cold sea.

Twenty-four years ago, the first signs
that you wanted to be out – a tightening
in the back and the feeling that I had to be
near water – this was where we came.

Today I sit much further out
on the blunt grey folds of rocks
which drowse like ancient elephants
under rugs of bright-green algae.

I'm remembering how heavily I trod
in my black cape around the lighthouse,
telling myself that if one bird
were perched on that obelisk in the sea

you and I and the birth would be just fine.
So what was I to make of three –
the cormorants – cramped in that narrow space,
no room to spread their wings?

Missing The Eclipse

for Anna

I'm lying on the bed that was your sister's, listening
to trains, wondering if they kept you both awake
while first your father and I, and then my lover and I,
slept on the side of the house which looks towards the sea.
It's cold in here. The curtain's torn, the double glazing
has a broken seal we should have fixed.
Through smears of condensation, the moon looks frenzied.

I'm thinking of what you told me in the bar tonight:
how you'd been unhappy in this house,
hating the slugs that came up from the sink ,
the grubby towels, the piles of washing in the shed
where your school shirt was hiding; how small
I'd made you feel, when you were small,
for caring, I with my eye on larger things.

The moon is shining straight into my eyes.
Outside the Underground, screaming at each other
among the late-night shoppers, why didn't we
look up and see its strangeness in the sky?
Then you walked away in your black coat,
looking so like my father's sister Ann
at her father's funeral that I called after you.

I wish that I could ring you and explain
that I know what has been missed.
That the dust and debris whirling round the earth
shut off the sun, distorting any light
which reached the moon, but only for a while.
That she's calmer now, although north of here,
in Turnhouse, they say she turned brick red.

Block

Inside me, an East European poet
is trying to get out. He's killing me,
and I, with my recurring ear-infections
and job, am slowly stifling him.

He has known political violence,
with neither mortgage nor menses
to distract him. He hates alliteration;
and strips his poems of accidental music.

A glass is a glass and bread is bread:
appearances keep us from the thing itself.
I've tried dropping the word 'quiddity'
into conversations to see where it might lead.

This isn't working, you and me.
You haven't written anything for months.

When the house is quiet, the phone not ringing,
I find his lines dangling like wire hangers,
with an austere beauty of their own.
I'm not sure what to do with them.

I keep up my pretences, adding to my stock
of special writing pens with different inks
and to the pile of notebooks by the bed.
I find the blankness of their pages soothing.

Blankness is the space around the poem,
the one you actually get down upon the page!

I stare at my screensaver of sky and clouds.
For translators, his brevity must be a gift.
Today I woke up from another dreamless sleep,
convinced that I should let his talent out.

Then he starts up: *Your problem, angel, is*
it's easier to love someone than be someone.

After that, as far as I'm concerned,
he can stay inside me. He can rot.

Standing Pose

for Sirkka-Liisa Konttinen

You told me that you dried yourself,
picked up your bag,
and climbed the steps from the small beach.
Then you looked back
and wished you had your camera:

the sun had blurred and a thick fret
rolled in towards me
standing on one leg against the sea,
foot tucked into my groin,
arms raised above my head.

I pictured the picture you would have taken
before I disappeared.
Woman Balancing in Light and Fog.
I felt rescued, centred by you
in front of water that still shone.

From The Fury of the Northmen, O Lord

In Denmark, your mother insists we run barefoot.
So every morning you sleep on
while she and I pound the cold hard sand,
jarring our spines under an iron sky.
The North sea snaps at my ankles,
which on day three swell up like mushrooms.

In the afternoons your parents stride ahead.
You are their long-haired Viking prince
and I your little mermaid, hobbling on knives.
You slow down for me, blank-faced,
when a one-legged sailor overtakes me
and thumps on crutches towards the dunes.

Your father's outburst over my eating salad
with my fingers cools and hardens. The sunsets,
he agrees, make up for everything.
Before the nightly board games, we stand
without a drink in hand outside the cottage
for the spectacle which the sky unfailingly puts on.

It only takes, in all the fiery-gold, one
darker fish-mail cloud, and there's his armour –
Svein Fork-beard, impaler of English women,
challenging his father Harald, son of Gorm.
Encased in iron and drunk as lords,
they're dragged beneath excited, bloody waves.

Keeping Them Out

Her mother's warned me that she's off her meds
and to watch out for the signs.
On the phone, her silence grows.
Then her polite young woman's voice:
it seems her angel Uriel thinks
I'm open to receive and should be fine.
She asks me not to drive, as it will make
the planet filthier and heavier with smoke.

Her room is in the dirtiest street,
caught between afternoon and evening
in the shadow of trees. The scent of jasmine
worries her– usually it's gone by noon.
She cuts cake, makes tea, as angels watch
from every wall. She's done as she was told:
given all her money to the poor, and thrown
her precious stones into the sea

but she's still afraid the dark ones
will get inside her head.
Kneeling at my feet, she lays out
a path of angel cards to where
only she can go, where branches twitch
and leaves are disturbed. Is there a poem
about a wedding ring? And do I ever
pray for animals? I say, *Yes,* and *Never.*

The Lost Ring Complains

Was it worth it, abandoning my Celtic knot

so that your wedding finger

could be nude and free in that slick water?

Why do you grub

so long in the hot sand to get me back?

Sweetheart, you didn't have

a chance. The marriage is gone, and you're left

to those three beauties

laid out to ripen under a blazing circle of Greek gold.

The bronze oil gleaming

on your daughters' thighs cost more than I did

twenty years ago

when the pair of you seemed to find

my silver lovely, and enough.

After Basho

Even when
the house is sleeping
and the poem
is almost here,
I long
for the house to be sleeping.

Safe House on Fourlawshill Top

for Peter Bennet

And finally the poets come,
driven by their muse or better half,
not to the usual distraction,
but to this place of whisperings and shades,
where poems are glimpsed only
from the corner of the eye,
cackling and vanishing round corners.

In modest cars they come
down unsuspecting lanes,
their glass-bowled offerings balanced
on their knees, wooed
by the symmetry of the hill's four laws:
Wit, Wisdom, Wantonness and Wine,
leaving behind town glasshouses
and dread of the sharp, flung stone
and the death of inspiration.

Eyes closed as the cars ascend the hill,
the poets dream they will be safe
a mile past midsummer lunacy at its height;
how at last they will expose
the thinnest of thin skins to a genial sun;
and later, kneeling by the pond,
reach to catch in white besotted fingers
the slippery fat orange of the moon.

Morphine

i.m. my mother, Flo Coventry.

60 grams

Your hand drifts in mine.
I kneel beside your chair
and your talk wraps round me
loose and warm, a stole
of slack knitting, dropped stitches
of which you'd be ashamed.
I can see the rims and sockets
of your eyes.

Later, I dream I squat
before the TV in your living-room;
punch each button.
And it stays blank.

220 grams

The telephone landscape was so familiar,
flat, negotiable, that I thought your will-power
and the old bearings would see us through.
But there was something different
in your voice that night, harsher,
almost irritable as you reined in sentences
that veered off the track. Then *lucid,*
you said, *lucid* – as if the word itself
were potent enough to bring you back
to tell me things were, honestly,
things were not too bad.

300 grams

Your hair smoothed back like that,
unusual, darker than grey with sweat,
your skull is fine and plain
for all to see, dreaming, twitching
on the cotton pillow.

Your eyebrow's warm ridge is there
to stroke with my forefinger;
and the fluid gathering in your hands
to ease upwards over your wrists
with baby-lotion.

Your elfin ear's upturned towards
my murmured, careful nothings.
Or I could hold my tongue and watch
the bate and catch of each long breath,
the eking out

of life and love and, through the window,
the shifting of the trees' white blossoms.

The Banner

I leave you with my brother
in the shadowed ward of women,
and find a morning, birdcalls

and the aching green of leaves.
I drive home through empty streets
as though carrying liquid

that must not be spilt.
In your cold bed, I roll
into the sag you made with your small weight

and sleep two hours;
then jack-knife from a dream
that you were shrinking back

from visitors who came and came.
I take a bath, and choose
a blouse the morphine will prevent you seeing:

white, sprigged with flowers.
I loop my hair in a young girl's band.
Behind me in the mirror, your dresses

cluster brightly on their hangers.
My hands and wrists are cool although the traffic
wavers in the heat. The red sandals

tread on daisies as I cross the lawn
towards the hospice breathing among trees.
I know you will have waited,

and would have smiled
at my bare arms and summer finery.
Out of the blue

and holding air
the thought unfurls–
A lovely day you've got for it.

The Stuart Bar, Liverpool

Light dirtied by the window falls on your white head ,
and I'm relieved that you still look the part,
your cap on the table, and your glass of bitter
almost empty. Against a backdrop
of frosted glass and gull-shapes swooping
for the chip-shop scraps, you sit alone,
in this bar you once jumped ship for
in the war, where women are still not welcome.
You, the golden boy, quoter of verse, teller of tales.
Your drinking friends long dead,
and the whiskies of respect no longer coming.
No-one smiles when I walk in and you jump up,
calling my name and fluttering your hands
before you like a girl .

By the time the neon lights come on,
showing up your trouser stains and dirty collar,
I'm your brand-new pal. I've fetched you
twice too often the cheap wine you switch to
after Bell's. I've been cold-shouldered
by the regulars at the bar, and heard enough
of Joe Louis and Dixie Dean, and blind Ray
at the next table who used to play for Everton.
I just want to get you home for food and a bath.
Which is your cue, to drop your voice an octave
and take us down into MacCaulay's *Lays,*
Virgil with a line-by-line translation,
Burn's *Afton Water,* or *Beautiful Dreamer,*
without a mention of her name.

Now you're spinning words for all that you
and I are worth, against the silent drinkers,
the TV blaring from the corner,
the crackhead selling T-shirts,
the karaoke squawking from the lounge.
You're my father, your head is close
to mine, and I am listening.

Lear's Only Daughter

You come visiting, Dad, with one small suitcase,
and without your riotous knights.

All ghosts now, your drinking-pals,
summoned up for stories in the grim bar

where you eke out your days.
Dead, you say, from too much abstention.

You see me, don't you, as your good girl
who sat your shift and mine beside her hospice bed;

who held your cold hand the night
when burglars carried off two coffee mugs,

a radio and your anniversary cassette.
But my voice was never gentle, soft and low,

and you won't wear your deaf-aid, will you,
to hear my stern complaints about the way

her hard-earned pension is disappearing
on Australian white. I need you

to liven up and get back
to the fine fettle of a rage,

throw my maths homework at me,
and call me thick.

This is no time to start telling me
you love me. I can see

where it's all leading.
Dad, this fifth act's no place for us.

Decent

i.m. my father James Coventry

You are decent in new pyjamas but only just,
with a blue sore on your lip I've not seen before.
This room where they have placed you is not enough:
a bed, window, chair, half-open door.

About four hours ago, they said, and lied.
Your forehead stings my kiss.
Which means the night-staff never checked;
left you unanswered, frowning, just like this.

Double Exposure

for John

You were driving us gently down the Dock Road,
past old strike graffiti and boarded-up pubs.
We knew those high walls and the streets running up
from the river, but somehow this felt like a trip –
the soft morning, or the camera my daughter
was holding, or the way you slowed down
to see basins containing nothing but water and light.

On the ghost tramlines at the edge of the city,
I said, *Somewhere green where we can still see the river*
and you found it: a space with huge clouds.
And because you're my brother who remembers all things,
who took 'Useless Facts' to the job in the desert,
I could pick up the phone and you'd tell me
if what you then took from the boot was an urn or a box.

I should know who dug first into his chill greyness,
if it scattered (was there a breeze?) or fell
in pale scythes on the grass. But I still feel the warmth
of your side, see your arm curving outwards,
and, when we turned back, Laura lowering her camera,
not knowing that she hadn't wound on, that we
would be tiny, bowed before three giant sisters
laughing at what we can't see, into the white.

Round Corners

The curtains she'd always hated flapped
their dirty beige-brown flowers
through broken glass out into the street.

The downstairs windows were boarded up.
Worse than the graffiti, the potatoes stuck
between each railing, sprouting insolent green.

Neighbours said the house was being used.
The letter-box snapped up onto a breathing
blackness, which no-one would call home.

She saw round corners. Where the sofa
had been, figures slumped against the wall.
Floorboards. Glistening fingers of burnt foil.

Daylight, and pigeon feathers were floating
down the stairs. Her mother was coming,
smiling, along the hall: *Alright, alright.*

Round the back, she climbed up on the wall
the way her brother used to. Spilt binbags.
Someone should have closed the toilet door.

A child was squealing. Dad was hosing down
her tiny self in the ruched swimsuit. Nothing
that a camera could take away. That fifties' heat-wave

The Maestro

It's you and that Charlie Gorse, heads
stuck up the chimney, coaxing down
the parrot you let out of the cage
for a bet on which way she would fly.
The bird's black as a crow and trembling
and Charlie says the wife will kill you both.
The bowl of water's your idea; but it's Charlie
who blow-dries the corpse and lays it
gently in the cage, begging you to stay
for one more drink, just till she gets home

I'm wearing your stories. They're big.
They hang off my shoulders and trail
in my soup. I don't care that the smiles
of those who outlived you are polite, even sad.
It's Pansy Street, the cart-horse drops dead
and you ring the undertakers with measurements
for a casket. I'm ignoring the child who says
Boring – it's engraved on my brain.
I'm raising my glass. We will hear it again.

Portuguese Blueprint

A man is slyly dipping his rod into the river. High on the stone terrace, his yellow sleeve and his hand curving round the rod are caught in her binoculars. When he leans forward, his dark head and the angle of his cheek are close to her face.

The house behind her is full of binoculars. The new window in the study frames the grey-green river and the brown fist of a hill just as the American had wanted. On the wall opposite hangs the original blueprint and land-deed, where the nineteenth-century river winds in Prussian blue on soft washed paper through a blue orchard with blue trees. In the bottom right corner curls the first owner's white, English name.

For days now, she has sat on the terrace, watching rain fall on the lilacs, dipping her pen into the American's landscape. At night, she lies on his bed, listening to fifties' jazz, and sipping rusty Dăo wine from the cellar.

Yellow Sleeve has put down the rod and lit a cigarette.

When she was a child, *river* and *orchard* were black on white in books that had to be returned to the city library. Yesterday she took off her clothes, intending to go down and swim. Instead, she knelt on the couch and rested her forehead on the glass between her and blue. If there were a fire, this is what she'd save.

The most protected river in Europe, according to João the gardener. Once, when he landed a trout at midnight to feed his family, he did forty days in Visĕu gaol. *The American's hardly ever here;* he said, handing her the key. *He'll never know. Be out by Friday.*

Yellow Sleeve has gone.

She lowers the binoculars. She wonders who is watching her. Tomorrow she'll give back the key

Evening, Unsettled

Draw curtains on the daffodil assaulted
by the blizzard against the garden wall, and sit.
Invent a ticking clock. Take out
your small, blue-veined imagination;
slip it into a bowl of water to sigh and settle.
Try on the promised quietude of middle age.

It's easier on the mornings that don't lie in wait,
when trees are filled with nothing but themselves,
when a black dog circles on itself
until it's whistled. Outside the trees
bang branches. The imagination whimpers.
Soothe it with the moonstone on your palm.

Your fingers uncurl like petals in your lap.
Contemplate the dried–out branch writhing
in the hearth. Don't play the song again –
Lanegan walking a mile for every year of his life
in the *fuckin'* stinking rain. He's half your age.
Remind yourself you're wanting to slow down.

Unsolicited Information

If you asked me what desire was,
I'd make a show of having to remember
the theatre in Skopje, three hours of darkness
the arm of the Macedonian touching mine.
And knowing what you can do with words, I'd imply
that the wetness between my thighs was quite
exceptional, because neither he nor Oedipus
had any language which could distract.
As you do now, describing the seal
the fishermen found on the pier, its round
bewildered eye, how gently they slid it
into the sea. Your hands warm the cup.
The next silence I can fill with that small cloud
being eaten slowly by the empty sky.

Firewall

Even my dreams are on guard against you.
A branch snaps back into my face
and bars me from the dripping forest
where dead pixels mean that you are lurking.
Or I swim through murky waters behind
a bluish shape which at the edge of sleep
turns, sways upright on leg-like fins
to just your height, and disappears.
Most mornings, though, I wake bone-dry,
a taste of metal in the mouth,
as if, instead of chasing the coelacanth,
I've been staring at the screen all night,
not trusting the latest downloads.
Versions of you still get through.

Worm

The dream recovers itself intact.
Waste ground: small fires are burning
and I'm huddled, a blanket folded at my feet.
Poems – mine – whirl past into the dark.
One catches fire and drifts around my head.
I see the line I know I have to hate.
I lie down and pull the blanket up.
A space opens under my left rib
where a warm thing is burrowing in.
Your hand is tracing my hip's curve, or
is mine tracing yours? *That was the line,*
you murmur. *Intercostally, I exist.*
You made me, which means I have to stay.
A second pulse beats faintly in my wrist.

Truants at Ironbridge

Hot morning on the river path
below the power-station's cooling towers.

Honeysuckle and stinkweed tickle
our bare legs; and the morning-glory gapes.

We're infants in the world's cradle of industry,
too tender for the Coalbrookdale Iron Museum

the Tar Tunnel, or the Victorian Town.
Your pink mouth exclaims at the yellow wagtail

opening and closing its beak on dry gravel,
I'm laughing and spitting out midges,

and the first iron bridge in the world hangs
upside down in the river's brown throat.

Boys Jumping off the Pier at Evening

They've given their light up to the day,
black shadows
jumping
one at a time
arms clenched to chest.

Fuckin' freeeeeeeeeeezin'

One stands apart,
thigh-deep and oiled by water.
Later, his girl
will touch his icy waist.

For His Parents

We went up one by one
and I saw the way she looked into each face.

I said that I had liked his poem
about their gardening in the dark together,
trying to save their plants from frost.

She was uncertain:
he had told them not to read his book
because it would upset them.
She asked me if I thought they should.

He looked at me, then at the ground.
I said that I had found this one
warmer, more affectionate than the ones
about his pain.

Then someone touched her arm,
she was looking up into another face,
and I was out of it.

The book was next to two of his CDs
on a table with the funeral card.
I tried to read the poem again

but single words had slipped their leash,
leapt viciously at my throat –
soil   *stiffening*   *silent*
– and would not lie down.

Just Another Mango

When at parties they asked me, leaning in closer,
why the marriage broke up/ the job didn't work out/
the daughters left home/ – they got what they wanted:
a tale with cause and effect, villain and victim,
to keep them nodding and murmuring, staring and whooping.

Years passed, and I gave a less muscular yarn,
with such texturing, such shy hesitations
over everyone's motives, shadows lengthening
on the high plain of hindsight, that they yawned,
Yes, how decent. (How boring. How tame.)

Now I tell them that the question left hanging is cleaner;
that I won't even *read* fiction; and to remember that life
is just mangos, some bursting with goodness,
waiting to be sucked; others turning to liquor. *Whatever,*
I smile, *wear white. Love those yellow, indelible stains.*

On Reading a Long Poem by a Younger Woman

In my garden, a woman is singing
a song of afternoon's end
and the gap before evening.

Her rich voice carries
to the stone bench where I'm lying
in the last oblong of sun.

The song is difficult, elaborate –
not one I 'd have chosen –
but I am glad she is singing.

The flowers on the trellis are scentless;
have been for some time.
From the terrace, I can't see her face,

only her colourless dress,
or perhaps it's the space
she furls round herself and her song.

Down on the lawn, my students
have packed up their books and clicked
their e-dictionaries to sleep.

They call to each other
in Mandarin and Thai, or murmur
into their phones as they drift away

over the grass, under her voice
which strengthens and soars
from the shadows, and falls

to the fishing-boats stuck
in the blue painted sea.
Their sails twitch and fret

as if she reminds them
of what they might do and where
they might go, but too late.

The flagstones are losing their heat.
My tongue's an old dog
lain down in the hearth of my mouth,

refusing to budge.
Hers will be agile and pink,
flexing with and against

the sounds from her throat.
A man has appeared on the steps.
Has he come to tell her

what she does best?
Will they sing a duet?
I will her to sing on

so that the unmoving bird
in the branches above me
might be shamed

into opening its small
wooden beak to praise absence;
sing night.

The Mother Hood

Why at her age she took to wearing it again
was anybody's guess, the blue silk
covering her head so that her face was gone.
Hadn't she said that the children staring in
at the windows of her dreams were no longer hers?
Time was theirs. It nuzzled them in winter,
and loped ahead on summer evenings.
He liked to see her frowning as she wrote,
or using his binoculars on birds
whose names he taught her.

She couldn't explain how its blueness
felt like grace, a falling away from sight
and his attention into her heart-beat, alert
to any sound an adult child might make.

Clay

Cliff-top again.
We're sitting near the edge on grass
and she's holding her first distance glasses
carefully in her lap. A small boat
inches across the green-grey sea,
and the herring-gulls do their diagonals.
But she's watching me,
and telling me she still needs space.

When she was three,
I came back from the phone to find her
staring across her bowl where
suddenly not five but nine
fat strawberries gleamed, and only one
in mine. I laughed, delighted
she was so passionate and sly; stopped
when she frowned as if I'd spoilt the prize.

I say *Of course,*
and she nods, relieved; or wary
of the diva in me who would fling
her arms up to claw down
a finite lump of grey, keep it moist
for her to prod and pull into something
that would not be her own,
taking up the space that only she can shape.

Canvas

In the priory ruins
the air is soft before the rain.
Good Friday tourists wander round the graves.

Their children's cries:
I could write them down
on this sheet of paper resting on my knees.

The breeze touching their hair.
A girl's chiffon skirt caught between her legs.
A boy firing a water-pistol at the sea.

This morning a tiny sound
tapped through my sleep.
Only a ring-toned starling

in the clean grey sky.
Your birthday soon
and you've asked me not to write.

What's a letter?
Answered or unanswered,
it's not a question.

I un-nail clichés –
hope   alright   miss –
and push them round in threes.

The boy is clinging to the grassy slope
which falls towards the rocks.
His parents are nowhere to be seen.

The space you've claimed,
smelling of bleach and spring,
is just there across the sea:

you, in the Indonesian shop
with your small list –
washing powder, yoghurt, cheese –

or in your Dutch interior,
before a fresh stretched canvas,
about to make your mark.

Triangle

In three corners of the evening
in the same city,
each of my daughters
unlocks her own front door

and closes it,
turning to greet
the quiet that flows down the hall,
the small mirror,

and herself as protagonist.
Beyond that, I can't see.
I know that what they send
is a necessary gift,

a triangle of silences,
cold steel and symmetry
I slip over my wrist.
How long they've waited for this.

Through the time of the family's
five-pointed star: two
for diversity – their father and I –
then one sister plus two,

numerical perfection
which kept the wolf from the door.
Through the time of the quadrant,
at sea, me at the wheel

keeping their three white faces
and the sun at my back,
using an obsolete brass quarter-circle
to find the North Star.

They saw before I did
that, in the absence of landmarks,
dead reckoning was called for
and boats of their own.

They have sent me my own idiophone
(*Even an idiot could play it,*
the nun told me at school)
and all the time that I need

to practise; make perfect.
Hold it up to the sky,
uncompromising, beautiful,
to frame a branch and the moon,

and I see them as new.
Strike one side with a spoon,
and all three vibrate,
pure and strong, on one note.

Reading Between the Lines

You finish in me, your mouth warm on my neck.
In the cold air, neroli and lavender from the burner
float before dark wood and mirrors.
You sleep. I tip the candles with a glass,
and hold one bare in my fingers up to the book

between the lines
to protect the green

The flame haloes phrases, and the text dissolves.
As I turn the pages on new constellations

the gasping silver
dogfish swinging

hot wax falls on my hand and I almost cry out.
It cools and flakes. A car shushes past in the lane,
and over the houses I now hear the sea.
Beside the darkening waves, a small bird
will be running in an almost straight line.

White

White's what you want:
a house, a lake holding the pale sky
steady for your midnight swim,
your feet ghosting through a garden
so long and dark that you forget it's yours.

It's too late.
It's your commedia dell arte smile
as you sip reception wine and tell the artist
how you love but can't afford
her 5' by 4': the White on White.

White must go on:
not as in the radiance of eternity,
but as towels kept separate for guests,
voile curtains blurring the yard's bricks
and the dustbin to ethereal.

It's the high ground:
watching snow drift across the rocks
and huddling with friends in last year's jackets,
playing Five Stones with your principles
until your fingertips turn white.

White is what you're not supposed
to write: the scar on his long thigh,
gored by a fence at the age of five,
where you sometimes lay your head
and show him, slowly, you are grateful.

New in Vilnius

I slipped away from you
down alleys, into courtyards

glimpsed from the street
where your camera was absorbing

cornices, stone angels, lines,
to stand and hear

the ramshackle, two-storey houses
breathing under wooden roofs

which did not shine.
A dog sometimes barked

but if no yard-light came on
there was the dark

and the shapes of living spaces
under the soft cloth of sky.

For moments at a time,
I could be new, coming back

to a room where the light
hanging over the table

was still a miracle,
the blank sheets of paper

used on one side, a luxury.
Under the small, smudged moon

a lover like you became
a possibility. And when you came

through the archway to find me,
I'd be inside,

warming my hands
on the green radiator,

as it gurgled like the river
against the cold.

Notes

In the poem 'The Lust Meadow', *morgenlatte* is colloquial German for 'morning hard-on'. A latte is 'a decent length of wood.' The poem quoted is Robert Burns, 'Coming through the rye'.

The song alluded to in 'Evening, Unsettled' is Mark Lanegan's 'Lexington Slow Down' from the album *Here Comes that Weird Chill.*